Ali

GW00656242

The Winding Road to God

Thoughts from the
Catechism of the Catholic Church

VERITAS

First published 1995 by
Veritas Publications
7-8 Lower Abbey Street
Dublin 1

Copyright © Alice Taylor 1995

ISBN 1 85390 264 0

Cover design by Bill Bolger
Printed in Ireland by Criterion Press Ltd, Dublin

In our kitchen the picture of the Sacred Heart hung in a sheltered corner under the stairs. The stairs sloped above his head and to his right, in a small, deep-set window, sat the radio and its two glass batteries. He had a very good viewing position from which he could keep his eye on all the activity in the kitchen. Through a window straight opposite him he could even look out into the garden, the yard and down over the fields. I think that where he was hung was not the result of chance but of careful thought on my mother's part – she felt that she needed back-up, to keep an overseeing eye on the kitchen, the garden and the farm and also on her unruly flock.

Over the years the face behind the glass yellowed with the smoke of the fire and every Saturday when the windows were cleaned the Sacred Heart also got a swish of a paraffin-oiled newspaper. He had a long thin face with a sad but kind smile and his hair came down over his shoulders, which made me think that he looked like my mother when she let her hair down at night to comb it before she went to bed. His hands were held out as if he were asking for something and I felt that he was asking me to be good. On two straight lines beneath him, our seven names were written in my father's handwriting. The last name on the list was Connie, but he was no longer with us as he had died when he was five. His death had left a huge gap in my life. My mother told me that Connie

3

was in heaven with the man in the picture, which made me realise that the man in the picture was pretty powerful.

Sometimes, late on a winter's evening, the turf fire sent shadows dancing along the low timber ceiling of the kitchen and then the little red lamp on the shelf beneath the Sacred Heart covered his face in a warm glow. When the first bluebells appeared in the nearby wood we picked a bunch and stood them in a jam pot on the shelf beneath the picture. These were followed by the primroses, then sweet rocket and after that the old deep pink roses that filled the kitchen with their rich musky smell.

We brought the face of the changing seasons to our Sacred Heart and in some ways he was part of the family circle. That Sacred Heart was my first awareness of the face of God. In the parlour we had another Sacred Heart that had come from America years previously – a mosaic in a gilt frame – but to me it was just a picture. That parlour Sacred Heart was a bit like the visitors who were entertained there; kept at a distance and definitely not family. The Sacred Heart in the kitchen, however, was part of our daily lives. A bit like the wire hook above his head that my father used as his filing system and the creamery book stuck between the banisters of the stairs. I knew that he was not the picture, just as my grandmother's picture was not my grandmother. But her picture gave her a reality in our lives and when my father talked about his mother who had died before I was born, it made her more imaginable. It was the same with our Sacred Heart. He was a guiding light in my mother's world

4

and she was determined that he was going to be part of ours as well. As the catechism says:

> Each believer is thus a link in the great chain of believers. I cannot believe without being carried by the faith of others, and by my faith I help support others in the faith. (*166*)

My mother certainly saw herself as a link in the chain of believers; in another section of the catechism I came on a passage which illustrated for me both my parents' source of faith.

> Created in God's image and called to know and love him, the person who seeks God discovers certain ways of coming to know him. These 'ways' of approaching God from creation have a twofold point of departure: the physical world, and the human person. (*31*)

My mother's way of approaching God would certainly have been the human person. In the catechism there is a beautiful passage:

> The *human person:* with his openness to truth and beauty, his sense of moral goodness, his freedom and the voice of his conscience, with his longing for the infinite and for happiness, man questions himself about God's existence. In all this he discerns signs of his spiritual soul. The soul, 'the seed of eternity we bear in ourselves, irreducible to the merely material', can have its origins only in God. (*33*)

My mother would never have sat down and thought all this out, and her only 'spiritual' reading was the *Messenger* and *Far East* and the *Irish Catholic* newspaper. But because she incorporated God in her daily thinking and prayer, he became part of her ordinary life. She was a serene person with great trust in God, which made her almost indestructible in my eyes. I associated her serenity with her closeness to God and so, for me, that became a desirable relationship.

My father's way of approaching God, on the other hand, would have been through 'the physical world'. Because he was a volatile man the changing face of nature suited his temperament. God to him was a bird in flight or a leaping trout. He found his God out in the fields in the wonders of nature.

> The Church is a *cultivated field,* the tillage of God. On that land the ancient olive tree grows whose holy roots were the prophets and in which the reconciliation of Jews and Gentiles has been brought about and will be brought about again. That land, like a choice vineyard, has been planted by the heavenly cultivator. Yet the true vine is Christ who gives life and fruitfulness to the branches, that is, to us, who through the Church remain in Christ, without whom we can do nothing. (*755*)

And St Paul says:

> Ever since the creation of the world his invisible nature, namely, his eternal power and deity, has been clearly perceived in the things that have been made. (*Rom 1:19-20*) (*32*)

So it could be that in my childhood I unconsciously absorbed the two different roads by which my parents were travelling towards God, the human person and the natural world.

> The world, and man, attest that they contain within themselves neither their first principle nor their final end, but rather that they participate in Being itself, which alone is without origin or end. Thus, in different ways, man can come to know that there exists a reality which is the first cause and final end of all things, a reality 'that everyone calls "God"'. (*34*)

In school I discovered that God had a rule book. We had catechism for a half an hour after lunch every day, and once a week a tall, red-haired priest walked from the local village to examine us on our catechism and to test our knowledge of God and, in the process, terrified the daylights out of us. God became a test of knowledge, and in learning all the rules and regulations I got confused. It was my father who put things in perspective.

'Learn the Ten Commandments', he advised. 'They came from God and they make sense. Everything after that are additions and most of it only succeeds in complicating what was originally a fairly straightforward plan.'

Over the years I have often thought of that advice and of his wisdom in turning on the BBC every Sunday morning while we were having breakfast before going to Mass. We listened to the Church of England service and my father advised us that we were all 'worshipping the same God but we are travelling by different roads and they are no better or worse than we are'. He would have been in total agreement with the extract from the catechism which answers the question 'How Can We Speak About God?'

> In defending the ability of human reason to know God, the Church is expressing her confidence in the possibility of speaking about him to all men... and therefore of dialogue with other religions, with philosophy and science, as well as with unbelievers and atheists. (*39*)

Living on the land and being close to nature my father realised that our interpretation of God was narrowed by our human limitations, and yet our very humanity was a common bond with God who became man. The new catechism tells us:

> Since our knowledge of God is limited, our language about him is equally so. We can name God only by taking creatures as our starting point, and in accordance with our limited human ways of knowing and thinking. (*40*)

On rare occasions in life – even in childhood – we are given experiences which transcend our 'limited human ways'. One winter's evening I went up in the early dusk to the field where my father was ploughing; I walked in the gap and there across the furrows of brown earth the man, the plough and his horses were silhouetted against the darkening sky. The last rays of the winter sun haloed these three in a fusion of soft light: I held my breath, afraid to intrude because I felt that I had come on a holy communion of nature, God and man. On that cold evening as I stood in a muddy gap that picture became printed on the back pages of my mind and formed the basis of an awareness of God in places that had nothing to do with questions and answers. He was out there to be found in aloneness. The catechism tells us that

> God, who 'dwells in unapproachable light', wants to communicate his own divine light to the men he freely created, in order to adopt them as his sons in his only-begotten Son. By revealing himself God wishes to make them capable of responding to him, and of knowing him and of loving him far beyond their own natural capacity. (52)

As I progressed through school I found a sense of God in many poems but the one which woke me up to this fact was 'I See His Blood Upon the Rose', by Joseph Mary Plunkett:

> I see his blood upon the rose
> And in the stars the glory of his eyes,
> His body gleams amid eternal snows,
> His tears falls from the skies.
>
> I see his face in every flower;
> The thunder and the singing of the birds
> Are but his voice – and carven by his power
> Rocks are his written words.
>
> All pathways by his feet are worn,
> His strong heart stirs the ever beating sea,
> His crown of thorns is twined with every thorn,
> His cross is every tree.

Finding God in poetry led me to the belief that God is centred in all creativity – which is not surprising since he is the Creator. Creativity is associated with writing and painting and other artistic pursuits but it is equally to be found in gardening, knitting, baking, woodwork and many other creative skills. The sight of my mother making a cake and kneading the dough with her hands and then flattening it out on the timber table always filled me with wonder. When she finally laid it in the bastable over the fire I felt that she had put a little bit of herself into it and yet had enriched herself in its making. Creativity is an inner life spring which needs an outlet. When we drew a bucket of water from the well in the field behind the house I knew that the lifting out of the water from the top of well led to the bubbling up of a fresher, cleaner supply from the bowels of the earth. Releasing the creativity within us creates cleansed inner depths, stimulates fresh supplies and satisfies the inner being. If the water wasn't drawn from the well it would have stagnated and gone sour. When there is no outlet for our creativity it breaks out in frustration and bitterness and dissatisfaction. Sometimes it takes a little self-discipline to make the effort to identify and channel our specific creativity. But the catechism tells us

> The 'mastery' over the world that God offered man from the beginning was realized above all within man himself: mastery of self. (377)

At Mass as children we sat through our fair share of long, boring sermons, but it would be fair to say that we did not listen very attentively. We always sat in a side aisle of the church and the opposite aisle had an overhead gallery. I loved watching the people file in and took special notice if any extraordinary hat made an appearance. The seat in front of us was usually occupied by a heavily made-up lady who covered her face with a black veil – which rather defeated the purpose of the make-up – but occasionally all was revealed. If the sermon was over-long, the veil was raised and running repairs were made to her face. I waited breathlessly every Sunday for this to happen, but it only happened during long sermons so, despite my anxiety to escape from the church, one part of me wanted the sermon to continue so that the veil would be raised. We were threatened under pain of excommunication by my mother not to react in any way to this lady's goings-on, so we sat there poker-faced, with our eyes riveted to the strange range of compacts that emerged from her handbag.

The only thing that I knew about the priests who said the Masses were their names, but one name in particular stands out in my mind. Our parish priest was in hospital and the curate told us one Sunday that during the previous week he had bought a little side table for the altar and paid thirty pounds for it. It was the first time ever that church expenses were accounted for off the altar and for some reason it made an indelible impression on me, so much so that even up to this day I always check when I call to that church, to see if the little marble table with the brass legs is still there. Even when other church furniture was swept away in a flood of post-Vatican II fervour, the little table held its corner. It was bought at a time when lay participation in the Church was practically non-existent, and the fact that the young priest told us about the small table and how much it cost made it a symbol of sharing. It was important to me that we belonged to the decision-making of our Church.

Every Sunday I felt in some inexplicable way that a miracle took place on that altar and, though I did not understand it, I still wanted to be part of it. It was many years later before the full wonder of the Mass came to me, but even then some of the mystery had seeped into my child's mind.

On sunny Saturdays we went into the musty confession box to rattle off sins. Sometimes I was not even sure that I had committed them but I felt that I had to make up a quota. I had no sense of love or forgiveness. I felt that God was a judge, preoccupied with sin and punishment, almost as if he was an accountant who entered my debits and credits as they occurred. He was far removed from the gentle picture under the stairs or the God who walked out in my father's fields.

Now when I go to the Sacrament of Reconciliation and see the difference in the whole new approach to Confession I feel that great strides have been made and that now the Church is much more in harmony with the loving attitude of Jesus towards sinners. The old harshness is gone and the Church is much stronger on love.

On Good Fridays our church became a sombre place. The sadness and bleakness of the crucifixion came down over me like a black cloud. The hurt and agony caused an ache in my heart and for me Good Friday was a cold, bleak day. Kathleen Tynan's poem

'Sheep and Lambs' has in its depths the cold bleakness of the crucifixion.

All in the April evening,
April airs are abroad,
The sheep with their little lambs
Passed me by on the road.

The sheep with their little lambs
Passed me by on the road;
All in the April evening
I thought on the Lamb of God.

The lambs were weary, and crying
With a weak human cry.
I thought on the Lamb of God
Going meekly to die.

Up in the blue, blue mountains
Dewy pastures are sweet;
Rest for the little bodies,
Rest for the little feet,

But for the Lamb of God ,
Up on the hilltop green,
Only a cross of shame
Two stark crosses between.

All in the April evening,
April airs are abroad;
I saw the sheep with their lambs,
And thought of the Lamb of God.

When exams came my way in secondary school I prayed diligently for a successful result. I knew, however, that my mother's prayers were more powerful than mine because she never doubted for one minute that God would not look after things in the best way possible. Like the apostle John my mother believed that

> We shall… reassure our hearts before him whenever our hearts condemn us; for God is greater than our hearts, and he knows everything. (*I Jn 3:9-20*) (*208*)

And also that

> God is Truth itself, whose words cannot deceive. This is why one can abandon oneself in full trust to the truth and faithfulness of his word in all things. (*215*)

When obstacles appeared on my path I used God as an emergency relief service and in between times I rattled off prayers at him. But some nights when I said my prayers I knelt on the low window-sill of the bedroom and, resting my hands on the open window, I had a sense of God out there in those shadowy fields and in the darkening mountains on the horizon.

Then we had a school retreat for the first time. The priest who gave it was a large, jolly Redemptorist called Fr Walsh, who opened a door into another chamber of God… love. I had never thought much about whether God loved me or not and the subject had never come up for discussion. But then, in my world love was not discussed very freely at the time. If you loved somebody you helped them but you did not verbalise it. 'Words are not enough – deeds are required' (*Mt 21:28-32*). But when this happy man talked about the love of God with great conviction it gave me food for thought, though the concept was a bit beyond me. Nevertheless, he set a seed in my mind and it grew and withered and grew again over the years. However, I was a long way from St John's declaration that

> 'God is love' (*Jn 3:16*). God's very being is love. By sending his only Son and the Spirit of Love in the fullness of time, God has revealed his innermost secret. God himself is an exchange of love, Father, Son and Holy Spirit, and he has destined us to share in that exchange. (*221*)

But Fr Walsh had opened a door for me to that possibility and when, a year later, our paths crossed again when he gave another retreat in the convent I was attending for my final year, he confirmed his previous theme. His happiness in his priesthood showed and his words about the love of God were convincing as he was obviously experiencing it in his life. They would not have carried the same weight if he had not been the living reality of his belief. Looking back I realised that he showed us that love was much better than fear. That light of love is glowing in the new Catechism.

In that convent I watched the nuns, women who had dedicated their lives to God. Some were not designed for the job but for others it had been the right choice and they seemed to be carried along as if God were giving them a piggy-back. The ones who really stood out were those who worked hard at it.

Whoever is called 'to teach Christ' must first seek 'the surpassing worth of knowing Christ Jesus'; he must suffer 'the loss of all things' …'in order to gain Christ and be found in him', and 'to know him and the power of his resurrection, and [to] share his sufferings, becoming like him in his death, that if possible [he] may attain resurrection from the dead'. (*Phil 3:8-11*) (*428*)

From this loving knowledge of Christ springs the desire to proclaim him, to 'evangelize', and to lead others to the 'yes' of faith in Jesus Christ. But at the same time the need to know this faith better makes itself felt. (*429*)

One of the heroic nuns for me in that convent was Sr Eithne, whose compassion, sensitivity and self-discipline in setting herself high ideals caused us to raise our eyes above our own immediate needs. She taught us that inner self-sanctification and improvement was an ongoing, attainable challenge and a base from which to fulfil needs other than our own. It was a high target but she believed that the young need high targets to stretch their wings. I carried with me from that convent a sense of self-worth and the knowledge that the road ahead would be difficult but that God and I made a strong combination.

The Word became flesh to make us 'partake' of the divine nature. 'For this is why the Word became man, and the Son of God became the Son of man, so that man, by entering into communion with the Word and thus receiving divine sonship, might become a son of God.' 'For the

Son of God became man so that we might become God. The only begotten Son of God, wanting to make us sharers in his divinity, assumed our nature, so that he, made man, might make men gods.' (*460*)

Armed with Sr Eithne's philosophy of life I went out into the workplace and, though I fell far short of her ideals, I still floundered on. The Mass and the sacraments were stepping-stones that helped me to keep in contact with God. Something in the Mass lifted my mind to a higher level and gave rise to an inner searching for a closer relationship at that level, though I had no idea of how to go about getting there. Confession was one of the steps that I took to get myself into a fit state to receive Holy Communion, which I felt was the gateway to that higher place. There were some things in the Church with which I was not very comfortable but it was still an avenue of light to God.

The Church is the place where humanity must rediscover its unity and salvation. The Church is 'the world reconciled'. She is that bark which 'in the full sail of the Lord's cross, by the breath of the Holy Spirit, navigates safely in this world'. (*845*)

But there came a period in my life during which I found this very difficult to digest, when I believed that the institution of the Church was far removed from the loving face of God. I felt that there was no place for lay participation and that the clergy were too preoccupied with changing altars around and not trying to reach out and help the people who filled those same churches. During this period I went to Lough Derg and while there I had a long argument with a priest who was on pilgrimage, pouring out all my annoyance about what I saw as the blindness of the Church to the needs of the laity.

'You really are very annoyed about this', he said.

'I am', I told him.

'Why don't you write it all down?' he suggested.

One evening soon afterwards I watched a priest in a black soutane walk back and forth outside a church, probably reading his office, and I wrote:

Back to Simplicity
Oh, dedicated churchman dressed in black,
What a mighty church is at your back.
We are taught that by your hand
We must be led to our promised land.
Jesus is locked in your institutions
Of ancient laws and resolutions,
Buried so deep and out of sight
That sometimes we cannot see the light,
Behind huge walls which cost so much
Where simple things are out of touch.
But could it be He is not within
These walls so thick, with love so thin?
Does He walk on distant hills
Where long ago He cured all ills?
Is he gone out to open places
To simple people, all creeds, all races?
Is Jesus gone from off the altar
Catching fish down by the water?

Is He with the birds among the trees
Gathering honey with the bees?
Could it be in this simple way
That God meant man to kneel and pray?
(from *Close to the Earth,* Brandon, 1989)

I vented my frustration with the Church on our curate who smiled sadly at me one day and asked,

'Did you ever think that we too are victims of the system?'

I had never actually thought of it like that, because I had seen them as part of the system and as propping it up. Soon afterwards he came to me and asked me to be a lay minister, as they were about to be introduced.

'No,' I told him, 'I just couldn't do that.'

'Well,' he said, 'you're a real hurler on the ditch! Forever telling us what is wrong and when we try to change things refusing to help.'

He was quite right, and there was then no answer to his request except 'yes'.

Being a minister of the Eucharist was a humbling and enriching experience, and the fact that the ministers rotated and spread throughout the parish brought the Church much closer to the laity. It was a positive step and it bridged a gap between the laity and the clergy.

But I was still searching for something within the Church that I could only find out in the fields and woods. I think that I was searching for the joy of creation, the joy of the resurrection. 'So that as Christ was raised from the dead by the glory of the Father, we too might walk in the newness of life' (*Rom 6:4*). And yet I was aware of people who had the joy of the risen Christ in their hearts. Uncle Jacky who lived next door was one of them and I watched him live a very ordinary life with a great sense of peace and joy.

> During the greater part of his life Jesus shared the condition of the vast majority of human beings: a daily life spent without evident greatness, a life of manual labour. (*531*)

In all the years that I knew him, Jacky worked hard. I never heard him say bad word about anybody and he always had a hand out to help a neighbour. He loved going to Mass and went up the hill to the church every morning whistling happily, and when, later in the day, he went up the hilly garden to feed his hens he was as much at one with his God out in his garden as he was in the church. For him there was no division between his morning Mass and the rest of his day. When he suffered greatly in later life and had to have a limb amputated his spirit was not broken and his love and trust in God seemed to transcend every hardship that came his way. Death held no fears for him and he certainly believed that

> Heaven is the ultimate end and fulfilment of the deepest human longings, the state of supreme, definitive happiness. (*1024*)

He left behind the glow of his love of God and he made heaven seem a little bit nearer to earth.

> Do not weep, for I shall be more useful to you after my death and I shall help you more effectively than during my life. (*St Dominic*) (*956*)

He was the first of his generation of the family to die and as others followed over the years familiarity never wiped the awesomeness off the face of death. When you are young you think that death in some way belongs to the old and that maybe as the years go on you will change and be prepared for it, but watching relatives grow old and die made me realise that as the end approaches nothing changes. You die just as you have lived.

> If you aren't fit to face death today, it's very unlikely you will be tomorrow. (*The Imitation of Christ*) (*1014*)

My father died in a matter of minutes after going to bed one night but my mother had a slow, painful leavetaking as the result of a stroke which kept her invalided for two years before she died. Once, as she commented on the difference in their departures from this world, she remarked with a smile, 'Didn't your father really get away with murder?'

Her comment made me smile and I said to her, 'If Dad was confined to this room for as long as you have been, he would have eaten a hole out through that wall!'

As my mother's end drew near she enjoyed singing happy hymns and one prayer in particular became her favourite.

> This is the day that the Lord has made
> And each hour will be blessed
> If you ask him for the strength
> To do your very best.
> Whatever path you follow

He'll be walking by your side
To be your source of comfort
Your friend and constant guide.
The Lord is understanding
His mercy will not fail,
His love for you is infinite
His goodness will prevail.
Remember this each morning.
And you'll not be afraid
To face with growing confidence
The day the Lord has made.

It was not a prayer that my mother had been familiar with all her life but a dear friend had given me a little booklet for us to read together. We had come on this prayer and my mother drew great comfort from it when days were long and wearisome.

Reason would tell us that there should be no sadness in the death of an old person who has had a long and reasonably fulfilled life, but reason and logic have very little control over deep-rooted emotions. Our parents are our tree of life and when they come down, it is only natural that our intertwined human roots are disturbed. Death will always make us look more intently at life.

At the evening of life we shall be judged on our love. (*St John of the Cross*) (*1022*)

On the evening that my father died I remember standing on the banks of the river at the bottom of our farm and watching the water. Eight generations of our family have lived on the banks of that river and my father had fished it all his life. Now they were all gone and as I stood there I thought how transient life is and how timeless is the flow of a river and how powerful and everlasting is God in his creation. My father knew every inch of that river and there were very few days of his life that he had not walked along its banks. As I stood there that evening it was as if part of his spirit was still in that river. He had been part of that place and some essence of him still lived on.

> There is a living water in me, water that murmurs and says within me: Come to the Father. (*St Ignatius of Antioch*) (*1011*)

> Our lives are measured by time, in the due course of which we change, grow old and, as with all living beings on earth, death seems like the normal end of life. That aspect of death lends urgency to our lives: remembering our mortality helps us realize that we have only a limited time in which to bring our lives to fulfilment. (*1007*)

A few times during my life I have found myself swimming against the tide in my efforts to achieve something that I had set my heart on. Despite all my best efforts I did not succeed. Maybe the time was not right!

No matter how hard I tried I could not make certain things happen but then at a later date the same things seemed to happen effortlessly. This made me realise that 'there is a season for everything, a time for every occupation under heaven' (*Ecclesiastes 3*).

I was usually so busy with my plans that I had no time to consider or even see God's plan which, when it unfolded, was much wiser and simpler than mine.

It could be that the time was right when I was asked to join a local prayer group. My initial reaction was very negative. I felt that it was not my scene – I had always considered prayer to be a very private exchange between God and me and the idea of being part of a prayer group made me feel decidedly uncomfortable. The strange thing was that the friend who asked me was, I thought, an equally unlikely candidate for a prayer group and I told her so.

'You've never been to a prayer meeting,' she said, 'and here you are sitting in judgment on the whole thing. Why don't you come and see and then at least you'd know what you are talking about.'

Another friend who had always been a bit of a wet blanket had started to attend the prayer meeting and gradually she had become a much more pleasant and serene person. This made me rather curious. I went along, determined not to be impressed, and I wasn't. I couldn't relax surrounded by people and I certainly couldn't pray – the whole experience was a bit of an ordeal. Before I left, however, one of the members asked me what I thought of it.

'Don't think that it's for me really,' I answered.

'Give it another week or two before you decide,' she said. A commitment was neither asked for nor given and I went home thinking that I would proba-bly not return.

Towards the end of the week that followed I went out for a walk one morning. The early morning mist still clung to the trees and I could see horses appear and disappear in the nearby fields through the drifting cloud. A cock pheasant crowed on the headland, his bright feathers contrasting with the dark green briar-covered ditch. I stood to listen and watch and a hare shot past, its speed startling me. The countryside was celebrating the birth of a new day. I stood with my eyes closed, the better to absorb the joy of creation that was out there on that misty morning. As I stood savouring my surroundings the focus of the prayer meeting came back to me. An awareness that there was a link between the presence of God in the group of people at the meeting and his presence in creation that morning came to me forcefully. It was the coming together of my two childhood worlds of God, my father's world of God in creation and my mother's world of God in the human person. I knew then that I would go back again.

I went back the following week with an open mind and, gradually, as the weeks went by I found that I too relaxed and lost my self-consciousness with the other people in the room and concentrated on the presence of God in our midst. The people there were totally relaxed and at peace in the presence of God and I felt included in the circle of prayer and meditation. A feeling of togetherness in prayer with the other members grew and became a bond that drew us all closer to God and to each other. They became an avenue of light on my road to God.

That hour once a week at the prayer meeting became a source of great inner strength. There I found the joy that I had always felt was part of the presence of God in his Church. In setting aside a time for meditation, praise and prayer it created a pool of peace that spread into everyday life.

> Christ provides for our growth: to make us grow towards him, our head, he provides in his Body, the Church, the gifts and assistance by which we help one another along the way of salvation. (*794*)

In the busy world in which we now live there is very little time to be alone with ourselves or God.

> How often would I have gathered your children together as a hen gathers her brood under her wings, and you would not! (*Mt 23:37*) (*558*)

We have no thinking time so there is no aloneness into which God can enter. At the prayer meeting that time became available and for one hour a week the everyday cares were put on hold, the burdens were shed and the peace of God flowed freely. It is difficult to detach ourselves even for a short while from our daily cares but when we set them aside even for a little while, we can come back to them stronger and they do not feel as heavy. I found that resting place at the prayer meeting. It became a little invisible power house in my life and the peace and trust in God that prevailed as we gathered weekly seeped out into everyday living. There is wonderful strength in knowing that you are not alone, that you have fellow travellers on the journey.

> For where two or three meet in my name I shall be there with them. (*Mt 18:20*)

This promise became a reality at the prayer meeting. I met there many people who were much more alive to and aware of the presence of God in the ordinary than I was and they wanted to share their awareness with others.

Lay believers are in the front line of the Church life; for them the Church is the animating principle of human society. Therefore, they in particular ought to have an ever-clearer consciousness not only of belonging to the Church, but of being the Church, that is to say, the community of the faithful on earth under the leadership of the Pope, the common Head of the bishops in communion with him. They are the Church. (*Pius XII*) (*899*)

The Bible was the main door into this new awakening to the presence of God in my ordinary life; one that I was very reluctant to open. But perhaps lazy is a more suitable word than reluctant and for the first few years of attending the meetings the only Bible reading I did was at the prayer meeting. Even though I found it interesting I still did not do it at home. I was not reared to Bible reading and considered it in some way as not relevant to my way of living. But because I saw that some of my friends were finding great joy and comfort in it I too was encouraged to begin. Thus are we helped on our journey by others and it is just as the catechism says:

Each believer is thus a link in the great chain of believers. I cannot believe without being carried by the faith of others, and by my faith I help to support others in the faith. (*166*)

Gradually I made my way into the Bible. I found some of it wonderful and some of it hard to understand. I savoured the bits that I grew to love and passed hurriedly through other pieces. My Bible knowledge developed with time. Take, for instance, the story of Martha and Mary which I have come to love. I think that there is a little bit of Martha and Mary in each of us – trying to get the balance right is an ongoing challenge. Like Mary, we need space to give time to God in our lives, but the world, as Martha found, has a tight grip on us and can sometimes choke our freedom and spiritual growth. It is almost as if the Bible links the word of God with our daily life. My father found God out in his fields, Uncle Jacky found him interwoven through his gardening, his love of people and his daily Mass.

Now I had discovered a group of people who had found God in the Bible and shared prayer. These people had a hidden treasure in their lives whose radiance shone out from them and now I could glimpse that glow. I was determined to make the journey although it is so easy to be discouraged by the uphill struggle and to be brought down by problems.

When faced with a problem that is too big to handle I go to Ephesians for courage and comfort.

> Out of his infinite glory, may he give you the power through his Spirit for your hidden self to grow strong, so that Christ may live in your heart through faith, and then planted in love and built in love, you will with all the saints have strength to grasp the breadth and the length, the height, and the depth; until knowing the love of Christ, which is beyond all knowledge, you are filled with the utter fullness of God. Glory to him whose power working in us can do infinitely more than we can ask or imagine. (*3:16-20*)

These last two lines give me the confidence to do things that are actually far beyond my own ability. A friend at the prayer meeting lives her life by this and she is a woman full of the love of God. She speaks of them as her passport to walk on water: 'Glory to him whose power working in us can do infinitely more than we can ask or imagine.'

I need this confidence in God's presence right now. At the moment I am working through a problem and it will need the power of him who 'can do infinitely more than we can ask or imagine' to bring me out the other end. God has not left me alone at this time and neither have his people. A community of Poor Clares and my prayer group friends are praying me through the difficulty and it is a great comfort to know that they have me in their prayers.

In some ways the Bible could be described as a travel guide to the next life. If any of us were contemplating travelling to an unknown destination and there was literature available about its history and the different routes available we would probably study it intently. We would like a few pointers on how to enjoy our journey.

The new catechism could be described as the map for that journey. It points out the pot-holes and the bad bends but it is full of wisdom and comfort . There are some yield signs, some stop signs and quite a few flyovers. But if, after all that, you fall on your face, you will find love and understanding. We are all companions on that journey, all going in the one direction and, hopefully, all arriving safely. It is nice to be able to read and come to know that we are not alone.

Reading the catechism made me realise that our Church is in the care of a loving and forgiving God, and no matter how big a mess we make of things he will pick us up and dust us down and put us back together again because we belong to him and his love is far greater than any wrong we could ever bring about. He would raise us up on eagle's wings if only we were prepared to fly.

As I look back from where I now stand on the winding road to God I feel that when I was in my darkest patches God was just around the corner. He was with me in the darkness too but I couldn't see him. Sometimes it is years afterwards that we see God's jigsaw fall into place, sometimes it never does so. I remember once saying to my mother when I was feeling very miserable, 'I can't pray , I'm too miserable.'

She smiled kindly at me and said, 'No need to pray now, what you are going through is a prayer.'

So maybe a lot of our journey on the road to God is a prayer – we may not be consciously praying but we are struggling, and that too is a prayer. We have the wonderful knowledge that at end of the road God will be there waiting with outstretched arms to welcome us home.

> Heaven is the ultimate end and fulfilment of the deepest human longing, the state of supreme, definitive happiness... Scripture speaks of it in images: life, light, peace, wedding feast, wine of the kingdom, the Father's house, the heavenly Jerusalem, paradise: 'no eye had seen, nor ear

heard, nor the heart of man conceived, what God has prepared for those who love him'. (*I Cor 2:9*) (*1024, 1027*)